Protein Bars for Snacks & Desserts

A Healthy Treat that Provides You with Plenty of Protein

BY: TRISTAN SANDLER

Copyright © 2023 by Tristan Sandler. All Rights Reserved.

ͻ☉☉☉☉☉☉☉☉☉☉☉☉☉☉☉☉☉☉☉☉☉☉ͼ

License Notes

Let's get right into it because I wouldn't say I like fluff (you will see this in my recipes):

You aren't allowed to make any print or electronic reproductions, sell, re-publish, or distribute this book in parts or as a whole unless you have express written consent from me or my team.

Why? I worked really hard to put this book together and, if you share it with others through those means, I will not get any recognition or compensation for my effort. Not only that, but it's impossible to know how my work will be used or for what purposes. Thus, please refrain from sharing my work with others. Oh, and be careful when you're in the kitchen! My team and I aren't liable for any damages or accidents that occur from the interpretations of our recipes. Just take it easy and stay safe in the kitchen!

Table of Contents

Introduction 5

   1. Orange dark chocolate bars 7

   2. White chocolate cranberry bars 9

   3. Chocolate chip bars 11

   4. Double chocolate bars 13

   5. Lemon chia bars 15

   6. Raisin cookie bars 17

   7. Peanut butter bars 19

   8. Pineapple bars 21

   9. Strawberry bars 23

   10. Pistachio bars 25

   11. Peanut butter protein bars 27

   12. Peanut butter banana bars 29

   13. Almond coconut bars 31

   14. Nutella bars 33

   15. Blueberry bars 35

16. Pecan date bars 37

17. Coconut bars 39

18. Chocolate almond bars 41

19. Crispy bars 43

20. Fruity bars 45

21. Chocolate Oat bars 47

22. Blueberry yogurt bars 49

23. Snickers protein bars 51

24. White chocolate almond bars 53

25. Chewy cashew protein bars 55

26. Chocolate chip cookie bars 57

27. Banana bread bars 59

28. Oat hazelnut bars 61

29. Matcha bars 63

30. Crunchy rice bars 65

Conclusion 67

Author's Afterthoughts 68

Introduction

Protein bars enjoy huge popularity thanks to their convenience. Some love them because they offer a variety of flavors while providing healthy nutrients. Others appreciate the fact that they are easy to make. For me, it is a fact you can prepare them ahead and have them ready for the moments you crave something sweet.

In our home, we always have a cookie jar filled with tasty and aromatic protein bars. I like to prepare a double batch of the recipe, so healthy snacks are available anytime. I always keep the jar on the counter, so everyone will intuitively reach the bars instead of digging through the pantry and reaching for the unhealthy snacks. But also, we like to include one bar in our lunchboxes to get through the day.

Protein bars are a great way to step towards a healthy lifestyle. Packed with nuts, seeds, and grains, the tasty bars are a must-have in our home. Do you want to learn the secrets behind preparing the best protein bars? Let's start this journey and go through the secret tips and tricks together!

1. Orange dark chocolate bars

A combination of orange zest and dark chocolate satisfies your sweet cravings. The recipe is ideal for dessert lovers that want to quit eating refined sugars. With flavor-rich nuts and a citrus aroma, this recipe is the winning one.

Time: 40 minutes

Servings: 10

Ingredients

- 2 cups Medjool dates
- 1 cup hazelnuts
- ½ cup walnuts
- ½ cup shredded coconut
- A pinch of salt
- ½ cup pumpkin seeds
- 1 teaspoon orange zest
- ½ cup sugar-free chocolate chips

Instructions

Start by removing the seeds from your Medjool dates. Cut them in half or use a straw to push them out.

Add the hazelnuts, walnuts, and coconut to a food processor and pulse for ten seconds or until they are finely chopped.

Add the seeds, orange zest, and dates. Pulse again to combine.

Line an 8x8 baking pan with parchment paper for easy removal and add the mixture. Spread it with a spatula and let it sit in the fridge for at least half an hour.

Remove from the pan and cut into strips. Melt the sugar-free chocolate chips in the microwave and drizzle over the protein bars.

2. White chocolate cranberry bars

With sweet Medjool dates and dried cranberries, this recipe is a must for dessert lovers. Combining walnuts, pecans, and sunflower seeds adds the extra protein and healthy fats you are after. It is a balanced snack or dessert to make it into your diet.

Time: 50 minutes

Servings: 10

Ingredients

- 2 cups Medjool dates
- 1 cup walnuts
- 1 cup pecans
- ½ cup dried cranberries
- ½ cup sunflower seeds
- 1 cup white chocolate chips, sugar-free if preferred

Instructions

Start by removing the seeds from your Medjool dates. Cut them in half or use a straw to push them out.

Add the walnuts and pecans to a food processor and pulse for ten seconds or until they are finely chopped.

Add the seeds and dates. Pulse again to combine. Stir in the cranberries.

Line a baking pan with parchment paper for easy removal and add the mixture. Spread it with a spatula.

Melt the white chocolate chips and pour over the mixture. Let it sit in the fridge for at least half an hour.

Remove from the pan and cut into strips.

3. Chocolate chip bars

A simple recipe that gathers the sweet flavor of dates and the rich chocolatey note is a match made in heaven. The almonds and walnuts add a rich flavor while bringing a nutrient-decadent dessert to your table.

Time: 40 minutes

Servings: 10

Ingredients

- 2 cups Medjool dates
- 1 cup almonds
- ½ cup walnuts
- ½ cup roasted peanuts, unsalted
- A pinch of salt
- 1 cup sugar-free chocolate chips

Instructions

Start by removing the seeds from your Medjool dates. Cut them in half or use a straw to push them out.

Add the almonds, walnuts, and peanuts to a food processor and pulse for ten seconds or until they are finely chopped.

Add the dates. Pulse again until they become mushy, and combine the mixture.

Stir in the chocolate chips.

Line an 8x8 baking pan with parchment paper for easy removal and add the mixture. Can top with additional chocolate chips if desired. Spread it with a spatula and let it sit in the fridge for at least half an hour.

Remove from the pan and cut into strips.

4. Double chocolate bars

The double chocolate bars are one of my kids' favorite recipes. The process is so simple, and we like to prepare it together. They love to measure the ingredients and toss them in the food processor. Add white chocolate on top and make swirls for a more fun experience.

Time: 40 minutes

Servings: 10

Ingredients

- 2 cups Medjool dates
- 1 cup walnuts
- ½ cup pecans
- ½ cup almonds
- A pinch of salt
- ½ cup unsweetened cocoa powder
- ½ cup sugar-free chocolate chips

Instructions

Start by removing the seeds from your Medjool dates. Cut them in half or use a straw to push them out.

Add the nuts and cocoa powder to a food processor and pulse for ten seconds or until they are finely chopped.

Add the dates. Pulse again to combine and create a sticky mixture.

Stir in the chocolate chips.

Line a baking pan with parchment paper for easy removal and add the mixture. Spread it with a spatula and let it sit in the fridge for at least half an hour.

Remove from the pan and cut into strips.

5. Lemon chia bars

The lemon protein bars are your next favorite, with a strong citrus aroma and healthy ingredients. I like to prepare a double batch of them and pop them in everyone's lunch box. Perfect snack to keep you full and keep you away from the snacks.

Time: 40 minutes

Servings: 10

Ingredients

- 2 cups Medjool dates
- 1½ cups almonds
- ½ cup walnuts
- 2 teaspoons lemon zest
- ½ cup chia seeds

Instructions

Start by removing the seeds from your Medjool dates. Cut them in half or use a straw to push them out.

Add the nuts and lemon zest to a food processor and pulse for ten seconds or until they are finely chopped.

Add the chia seeds and dates. Pulse again to combine.

Line a baking pan with parchment paper for easy removal and add the mixture. Spread it with a spatula and let it sit in the fridge for at least half an hour.

Remove from the pan and cut into strips.

6. Raisin cookie bars

The raisin cookie protein bars are a healthy alternative to the classic recipe. I love how it keeps the same aroma while providing nutrients.

Time: 40 minutes

Servings: 10

Ingredients

- 2 cups Medjool dates
- 1 cup walnuts
- 1 cup almonds
- ½ cup raisins
- ¼ cup chia seeds
- 1 teaspoon cinnamon
- 1 teaspoon nutmeg

Instructions

Start by removing the seeds from your Medjool dates. Cut them in half or use a straw to push them out.

Add the almonds and walnuts to a food processor and pulse for ten seconds or until they are finely chopped.

Next, add the seeds and dates. Pulse again to combine. Stir in the raising so they remain whole. Don't pulse them since they will get shredded.

Line a baking pan with parchment paper for easy removal and add the mixture. Spread it with a spatula and let it sit in the fridge for at least half an hour.

Remove from the pan and cut into strips.

7. Peanut butter bars

Preparing protein bars is a fun experience for everyone. You don't need to have any culinary skills at all. I love this recipe because you can toss everything in your high-speed blender or food processor, and it does the magic. Pick the unsalted peanut for this recipe to get the right flavor.

Time: 40 minutes

Servings: 10

Ingredients

- 2 cups Medjool dates
- 1 cup walnuts
- ½ cup almonds
- ½ cup roasted peanuts, unsalted
- A pinch of salt
- ½ cup peanut butter, creamy and unsalted

Instructions

Start by removing the seeds from your Medjool dates. Cut them in half or use a straw to push them out.

Add the walnuts, almonds, and peanuts to a food processor and pulse for ten seconds or until they are finely chopped.

Add the peanut butter and dates. Pulse again to combine.

Line a baking pan with parchment paper for easy removal and add the mixture. Spread it with a spatula and let it sit in the fridge for at least half an hour.

Remove from the pan and cut into strips.

8. Pineapple bars

Adding dry fruits brings a ton of flavor to your recipe. Honestly, I find the combination of nuts and seeds pretty plain. Add dried pineapple and white chocolate to the basic recipe, and you have an exotic flavor on your plate.

Time: 40 minutes

Servings: 10

Ingredients

- 2 cups Medjool dates
- 1 cup almonds
- ½ cup walnuts
- ½ cup pecans
- ½ cup dried pineapple, finely chopped
- 1 cup white chocolate chips, sugar-free if preferred

Instructions

Start by removing the seeds from your Medjool dates. Cut them in half or use a straw to push them out.

Add the nuts to a food processor and pulse for ten seconds or until they are finely chopped.

Add the dates. Pulse again to combine. Stir in the dried pineapple so it stays in chunks.

Line a baking pan with parchment paper for easy removal and add the mixture. Spread it with a spatula and let it sit in the fridge for at least half an hour.

Remove from the pan and cut into strips. Melt the chocolate chips and drizzle the pineapple bars.

9. Strawberry bars

This recipe is an excellent way to use the dried strawberries left over in your pantry. I like adding some macadamia nuts to these protein bars to get the rich flavor. The vanilla extract adds an extra flavor and aroma, making you feel like you are eating a decadent dessert in your favorite bakery.

Time: 40 minutes

Servings: 10

Ingredients

- 2 cups Medjool dates
- 1 cup almonds
- ½ cup hazelnuts
- ½ cup macadamia nuts
- 1 teaspoon pure vanilla extract
- ½ cup pumpkin seeds
- ½ cup dried strawberries finely chopped

Instructions

Start by removing the seeds from your Medjool dates. Cut them in half or use a straw to push them out.

Add the nuts to a food processor and pulse for ten seconds or until they are finely chopped.

Add the seeds and dates. Pulse again to combine. Stir in the chopped dried strawberries.

Line a baking pan with parchment paper for easy removal and add the mixture. Spread it with a spatula and let it sit in the fridge for at least half an hour.

Remove from the pan and cut into strips.

10. Pistachio bars

Pistachios are an excellent addition to elevate your recipe. Despite adding authentic flavor, they will bring a pop of color. The chocolate chips complete the picture with the chocolatey flavor, creating a flawless combination that satisfies your cravings.

Time: 40 minutes

Servings: 10

Ingredients

- 2 cups Medjool dates
- 1 cup almonds
- 1 cup pecans
- ½ cup roughly chopped pistachios
- ½ cup mini chocolate chips

Instructions

Start by removing the seeds from your Medjool dates. Cut them in half or use a straw to push them out.

Add the almonds and pecans to a food processor and pulse for ten seconds or until they are finely chopped.

Add the dates and pistachios. Pulse again to combine. Stir in the chocolate chips.

Line a baking pan with parchment paper for easy removal and add the mixture. Spread it with a spatula and let it sit in the fridge for at least half an hour.

Remove from the pan and cut into strips.

11. Peanut butter protein bars

The simple combinations work best when it comes to protein bars. Adding rolled oats to your ingredient list boosts the protein content and ensures you feel full until lunchtime. I like to have this as breakfast when I don't feel like eating the same oat porridge.

Time: 40 minutes

Servings: 10

Ingredients

- 3/4 cup peanut butter softened at room temperature
- ½ cup honey
- ½ cup vanilla protein powder
- 1 ½ cups rolled oats
- ¼ cup dark sugar-free chocolate chips

Instructions

Add the honey and peanut butter to a large mixing bowl and combine.

Add the oats and mix well.

Sprinkle the protein powder and mix to combine. Stir in the chocolate chips.

Line a baking pan with parchment paper for easy removal and add the mixture. Spread it with a spatula and let it sit in the fridge for at least half an hour.

Remove from the pan and cut into strips.

12. Peanut butter banana bars

Now is the right time to use the overripe bananas you keep putting away to make banana bread. The combination of peanut butter and banana works every time. It is a flavor familiar to children, so it is more likely they will enjoy it.

Time: 1 hour 10 minutes

Servings: 10

Ingredients

- 1 3/4 cups rolled oats
- 3/4 cup peanut butter
- 1/3 cup agave
- 1 ripe banana, mashed
- ½ cup ground flax seed
- 2 teaspoons pure vanilla extract
- Pinch of salt
- 1 cup protein powder
- 3/4 cup mini chocolate chips, sugar-free if desired

Instructions

Add all of the ingredients for your protein bars into a mixing bowl. Stir well to combine them.

The mashed banana and honey should be enough to make the mixture stick but feel free to add a little more if it is too dry.

Line an 11x7 pan with parchment paper for easy removal and add the mixture. Spread it with a spatula and let it sit in the fridge for at least an hour.

Remove from the fridge and cut into strips.

13. Almond coconut bars

The almond coconut bars are simple yet versatile. If you have a healthy foodie in your life, a homemade batch of these would be the perfect gift. Pack them nicely, add a decorative ribbon, and be sure they will appreciate the homemade gift.

Time: 1 hour 10 minutes

Servings: 10

Ingredients

- 1 3/4 cups rolled oats
- 3/4 cup almond butter
- 1/3 cup honey, agave, or real maple syrup
- 1 ripe banana, mashed
- ½ cup ground flax seed
- Pinch of salt
- 2 teaspoons vanilla extract
- 1 cup protein powder
- 3/4 cup coconut flakes
- 2 cups unsweetened white chocolate chips, if desired, for topping

Instructions

Add all of the ingredients for your protein bars into a mixing bowl. Stir well to combine them.

The mashed banana and honey should be enough to make the mixture stick but feel free to add a little more if it is too dry.

Line an 11x7 pan with parchment paper for easy removal and add the mixture. Spread it with a spatula and let it sit in the fridge for at least an hour.

Remove from the fridge and cut into strips. Dip them in melted white chocolate if desired.

14. Nutella bars

Everyone loves the combination of rich chocolate and hazelnuts. But we know that store-bought one is packed with unhealthy fats and sugars. The cocoa powder and hazelnut butter help achieve the same flavor while cutting down unhealthy carbs and fats. I like to dip the whole bars in chocolate and pack them in my lunchbox for those emergency cravings.

Time: 1 hour 10 minutes

Servings: 10

Ingredients

- 1 3/4 cups rolled oats
- 3/4 cup hazelnut butter
- 1/3 cup maple syrup
- 1 ripe banana, mashed
- ½ cup ground flax seed
- Pinch of salt
- 4 tablespoons unsweetened cocoa powder
- 1 cup protein powder
- 3/4 cup chopped hazelnuts

Instructions

Add all of the ingredients for your protein bars into a mixing bowl. Stir well to combine them.

The mashed banana and honey should be enough to make the mixture stick but feel free to add a little more if it is too dry.

Line an 11x7 pan with parchment paper for easy removal and add the mixture. Spread it with a spatula and let it sit in the fridge for at least an hour.

Remove from the fridge and cut into strips.

15. Blueberry bars

What I love the most about protein bars is that they don't require baking. This makes the process more straightforward. I wasn't strictly limited to nuts and chocolate when experimenting with various flavors. Fruits can add a touch of freshness to your protein bars, so feel free to add some. Died blueberries bring the original berry flavor for tasty and healthy bars.

Time: 1 hour 10 minutes

Servings: 10

Ingredients

- 1 3/4 cups rolled oats
- 3/4 cup sunflower seed butter
- 1/3 cup honey
- 1 ripe banana, mashed
- ½ cup ground flax seed
- 2 teaspoons vanilla extract
- 1 cup vanilla protein powder
- 3/4 cup dried blueberries

Instructions

Add all of the ingredients for your protein bars into a mixing bowl. Stir well to combine them.

The mashed banana and honey should be enough to make the mixture stick but feel free to add a little more if it is too dry.

Line an 11x7 pan with parchment paper for easy removal and add the mixture. Spread it with a spatula and let it sit in the fridge for at least an hour.

Remove from the fridge and cut into strips. Dip our protein bars in melted chocolate if desired.

16. Pecan date bars

Pecans have a robust nutty flavor that stands out in recipes. These protein bars have a perfect combination of ingredients to get the best pecan flavor. If you're preparing a large batch for the month, feel free to freeze them.

Time: 1 hour 10 minutes

Servings: 10

Ingredients

- 1 3/4 cups rolled oats
- 3/4 cup pecan butter
- 1/3 cup agave
- 1 ripe banana, mashed
- ½ cup ground flax seed
- 2 teaspoons pure vanilla extract
- 1 cup chocolate protein powder
- 3/4 cup chopped dates

Instructions

Add all of the ingredients for your protein bars into a mixing bowl. Stir well to combine them.

The mashed banana and honey should be enough to make the mixture stick but feel free to add a little more if it is too dry.

Line an 11x7 pan with parchment paper for easy removal and add the mixture. Spread it with a spatula and let it sit in the fridge for at least an hour.

Remove from the fridge and cut into strips.

17. Coconut bars

The protein bar recipe will amaze all the coconut lovers out there. The secret trick is to use creamy coconut butter that does all the work. If you are one of the homemade nut butter people, you can make your coconut butter at home. Add the shredded coconut into a high-speed blender and wait until it releases the oils.

Time: 1 hour 10 minutes

Servings: 10

Ingredients

- 1 3/4 cups rolled oats
- 3/4 cup coconut butter
- 1/3 cup honey
- 1 ripe banana, mashed
- ½ cup ground flax seed
- Pinch of salt
- 2 teaspoons vanilla extract
- 1 cup protein powder
- 3/4 cup unsweetened coconut flakes
- 2 cups sugar-free white chocolate chips

Instructions

Add all of the ingredients for your protein bars into a mixing bowl. Stir well to combine them.

The mashed banana and honey should be enough to make the mixture stick but feel free to add a little more if it is too dry.

Line an 11x7 pan with parchment paper for easy removal and add the mixture. Spread it with a spatula and let it sit in the fridge for at least an hour.

Remove from the fridge and cut into strips. Melt the chocolate chips and dip the coconut bars if desired.

18. Chocolate almond bars

The chocolate almond bars are your go-to recipe when you crave sweets. Keep them within arms reach to avoid the unhealthy desserts in your pantry.

Time: 1 hour 10 minutes

Servings: 10

Ingredients

- 1 3/4 cups rolled oats
- ½ cup ground flax seed
- 3/4 cup almond butter
- 1/3 cup honey, agave, or real maple syrup
- 1 ripe banana, mashed
- Pinch of salt
- 2 tablespoons unsweetened cocoa powder
- 1 cup protein powder
- 3/4 cup chopped almonds

Instructions

Add all of the ingredients for your protein bars into a mixing bowl. Stir well to combine them.

The mashed banana and honey should be enough to make the mixture stick but feel free to add a little more if it is too dry.

Line an 11x7 pan with parchment paper for easy removal and add the mixture. Spread it with a spatula and let it sit in the fridge for at least an hour.

Remove from the fridge and cut into strips.

19. Crispy bars

When you want to opt for a lighter option without strong nut flavor, go for the crispy bars. The addition in this recipe adds crunchiness and contributes to a more delicate flavor. Perfect for your picky eaters that find the nut flavor to be too strong for them.

Time: 1 hour 10 minutes

Servings: 10

Ingredients

- 1 3/4 cups rolled oats
- 3/4 cup macadamia butter
- 1/3 cup agave
- 1 ripe banana, mashed
- ½ cup ground flax seed
- Pinch of salt
- 2 teaspoons vanilla extract
- 1 cup protein powder
- 3/4 cup crispy rice cereal

Instructions

Add all of the ingredients for your protein bars into a mixing bowl. Stir well to combine them.

The mashed banana and honey should be enough to make the mixture stick but feel free to add a little more if it is too dry.

Line an 11x7 pan with parchment paper for easy removal and add the mixture. Spread it with a spatula and let it sit in the fridge for at least an hour.

Remove from the fridge and cut into strips.

20. Fruity bars

If you don't like the intense taste of oats, try to conceal it with fruits and nuts. The honey and mashed banana help to create a sticky mixture, while the chopped dried fruits add flavor. Feel free to use a fruit mix that suits your taste. I love this recipe's papaya and pineapple combination, but you can switch them if you like.

Time: 1 hour 10 minutes

Servings: 10

Ingredients

- 1 3/4 cups rolled oats
- 3/4 cup coconut butter
- 1/3 cup honey
- 1 ripe banana, mashed
- ½ cup ground flax seed
- 2 teaspoons vanilla extract
- 1 cup protein powder
- 3/4 cup chopped mix of dry exotic fruits (pineapple, papaya, mango, etc.)

Instructions

Add all of the ingredients for your protein bars into a mixing bowl. Stir well to combine them.

The mashed banana and honey should be enough to make the mixture stick but feel free to add a little more if it is too dry.

Line an 11x7 pan with parchment paper for easy removal and add the mixture. Spread it with a spatula and let it sit in the fridge for at least an hour.

Remove from the fridge and cut into strips.

21. Chocolate Oat bars

If you want to have different flavors, try switching your sweetener options. I like using whole dates as a sweetener in most recipes. Sometimes I change it with honey to alter the flavor. Date syrup is another excellent alternative that brings a hint of caramel to your recipe.

Time: 40 minutes

Servings: 10

Ingredients

- 1 cup rolled oats
- 1/3 cup chocolate protein powder
- ¼ cup mini chocolate chips
- ½ cup creamy peanut butter
- 3 tablespoons date syrup
- 3 teaspoons water

Instructions

Add all of the ingredients for your protein bars into a mixing bowl. Stir well to combine them. Add some more water if the protein bar mixture appears too dry.

Line a pan with parchment paper for easy removal and add the mixture. Spread it with a spatula and let it sit in the fridge for at least an hour.

22. Blueberry yogurt bars

If you're looking for a protein bar recipe different from the standard ones, you have found it. Combining green yogurt, almond, and coconut flour creates a decadent dessert for your enjoyment.

Time: 40 minutes

Servings:5

Ingredients

- 1 cup sweetened vanilla protein powder (can add granulated sweetener if using non sweetened powder)
- ¼ cup Greek yogurt
- ¼ cup almond flour
- ½ cup coconut flour
- 1/3 cup blueberry puree
- 2/3 cup sugar-free white chocolate chips
- 2 teaspoons coconut oil

Instructions

Add the protein powder, greek yogurt, coconut flour, almond flour, and blueberry puree in a mixing bowl. Mix well until combined. Line a baking pan with parchment paper for easy removal and add the mixture. Spread it with a spatula and let it sit in the fridge for at least half an hour.

Remove and cut into bars.

Melt the coconut oil and chocolate chips. Dip the yogurt bars in white chocolate and let it set.

23. Snickers protein bars

The peanut butter and chocolate recreate the authentic Snickers bar flavor while keeping it sugar-free. The recipe is enough for five bars, but feel free to double or triple the ingredients because they are a real delicacy.

Time: 40 minutes

Servings: 5

Ingredients

- 1 ½ cups peanut butter
- 3/4 cup protein powder
- ¼ cup honey
- Pinch of salt
- 4 oz chocolate chips
- 2 teaspoons coconut oil

Instructions

Mix the peanut butter, protein powder, honey, and salt until combined.

Line a baking pan with parchment paper for easy removal and add the mixture. Spread it with a spatula.

Melt the coconut oil and chocolate chips in your microwave. Spread over the mixture and let it sit in the fridge for at least half an hour.

Slice into bars and enjoy.

24. White chocolate almond bars

One of the ways to make protein bars is to use protein powder. You can use plain or flavored protein powder in your recipes. However, make sure to mind the sweetness. If your protein powder is already sweetened, you would want to omit to add sweetener to your recipe.

Time: 40 minutes

Servings: 5

Ingredients

- 1 ½ cups almond butter
- 3/4 cup vanilla protein powder
- ¼ cup agave (omit if your protein powder is sweetened)
- Pinch of salt
- 4 oz sugar-free white chocolate chips
- 2 teaspoons coconut oil

Instructions

Mix the butter, protein powder, agave, and salt until combined.

Line a baking pan with parchment paper for easy removal and add the mixture. Spread it with a spatula.

Melt the coconut oil and white chocolate chips in your microwave. Spread over the mixture and let it sit in the fridge for at least half an hour.

Slice into bars and enjoy.

25. Chewy cashew protein bars

The recipes with nut butters and protein powder are chewy and decadent, a perfect alternative for the crunchy nut-rich ones. Cashew butter is a more subtle option with no prominent nut flavor. Paired with chocolate, it is a combination that creates a decadent dessert.

Time: 40 minutes

Servings: 5

Ingredients

- 1 ½ cups cashew butter
- 3/4 cup chocolate protein powder
- ¼ cup maple syrup
- Pinch of salt
- 4 oz dark chocolate chips
- 2 teaspoons coconut oil

Instructions

Mix the butter, protein powder, maple syrup, and salt until combined.

Line a baking pan with parchment paper for easy removal and add the mixture. Spread it with a spatula.

Melt the chocolate chips and coconut oil in your microwave. Spread over the mixture and let it sit in the fridge for at least half an hour.

Slice into bars and enjoy.

26. Chocolate chip cookie bars

With only a few ingredients, this chocolate chip bar recipe is simple but never fails to amaze with its flavor. You can switch the agave with honey or another sweetener of your preference.

Time: 40 minutes

Servings: 10

Ingredients

- 1 ½ cups almond butter
- 3/4 cup chocolate protein powder
- ¼ cup agave
- Pinch of salt
- 2 oz mini chocolate chips, sugar-free version

Instructions

Mix the butter, protein powder, agave, and salt until combined. Stir in the mini chocolate chips.

Line a baking pan with parchment paper for easy removal and add the mixture. Spread it with a spatula. Let the protein bar mixture sit in the fridge for at least half an hour.

Slice into bars and enjoy.

27. Banana bread bars

This recipe recreates the classic flavors with a ripe banana, cinnamon, and nutmeg. Ideal for cold days when you want to comfort yourself with an aromatic dessert.

Time: 40 minutes

Servings: 10

Ingredients

- 1 ½ cups peanut butter
- 3/4 cup protein powder
- ¼ cup mashed ripe banana
- 1 teaspoon cinnamon
- 1 teaspoon nutmeg
- Pinch of salt
- 4 oz white chocolate chips
- 2 teaspoons coconut oil

Instructions

Mix the peanut butter, protein powder, banana, and salt until combined.

Line a baking pan with parchment paper for easy removal and add the mixture. Spread it with a spatula.

Melt the coconut oil and chocolate chips in your microwave. Spread over the mixture and let it sit in the fridge for at least half an hour.

Slice into bars and enjoy.

28. Oat hazelnut bars

Oats are a primary ingredient that can be used in so many flavor combinations. I used hazelnut butter and oat flour, enhanced by dark chocolate.

Time: 40 minutes

Servings: 10

Ingredients

- 1 ½ cups hazelnut butter
- 1 cup oat flour
- 1/3 cup honey
- Pinch of salt
- 4 oz dark chocolate chips
- 2 teaspoons coconut oil

Instructions

Mix the peanut butter, protein powder, honey, and salt until combined.

Line a baking pan with parchment paper for easy removal and add the mixture. Spread it with a spatula.

Melt the chocolate chips and coconut oil in your microwave. Spread over the mixture and let it sit in the fridge for at least half an hour.

Slice into bars and enjoy.

29. Matcha bars

If you're the type of person that adds matcha to anything, this recipe will exceed your expectations. Add only two tablespoons to get the rich matcha flavor and gorgeous green color.

Time: 40 minutes

Servings: 12

Ingredients

- 1 ¾ cups oat flour
- 2 tablespoon matcha green tea powder
- ½ cup vanilla protein powder
- Pinch of salt
- ½ cup almond butter
- ⅓ cup honey
- 1 teaspoon pure vanilla extract
- ¼ cup almond milk

Instructions

Add the pat flour, matcha, protein powder, and salt into a mixing bowl. Stir to combine.

Add in the almond butter, vanilla, milk, and honey. Mix well to combine.

Line a baking pan with parchment paper for easy removal and add the mixture. Spread it with a spatula and let it sit in the fridge for at least half an hour.

Remove from the pan and cut into strips. Drizzle with melted chocolate if desired, and let it set.

30. Crunchy rice bars

The crunchy rice cereal is perfect if you prefer a lighter flavor. In combination with cashew butter, it creates the ideal balance.

Time: 1 hour 10 minutes

Servings: 20

Ingredients

- 4 cups Brown Rice Cereal
- 1 cup cashew butter
- ½ cup protein powder
- 1 cup honey or another sweetener of your preference
- 2 cups sugar-free free chocolate chips
- 2 teaspoons coconut oil

Instructions

Melt the cashew butter and honey in a pot. Mix well and add the cereal and protein powder.

Line an 8x8 baking pan with parchment paper for easy removal and add the mixture. Spread it with a spatula and let it sit in the fridge for at least half an hour.

Melt the coconut oil and chocolate chips. Dip each bar and let it set.

Conclusion

After discovering my fabulous protein bar recipes, you can prepare your own. The process is straightforward and won't take much of your precious time. Prepare a large batch ahead and have a healthy snack within arm's reach to prevent you from picking the unhealthy treat choices.

Now that you know the basics, you can even step forward and customize the recipes. Follow your family's preferences and create your own custom recipe that fits your taste. It is a fun process that makes healthy food more fun.

I hope my curated recipes helped you develop healthy and mindful eating habits. My collection has plenty of healthy and simple recipes, so don't mind checking them out!

Author's Afterthoughts

thank you

Now's the moment of truth… What did you think about my cookbook? Did you like the recipes in it? While I certainly hope so, I would also like to know what you'd like to see more of! This might come as a surprise to you, but your ideas will surely inspire my upcoming cookbooks since the only reason I write is so that you can try out my dishes! Without you, I certainly wouldn't be here–writing and all.

Perhaps you'd like a cookbook to help you with weight loss or to help you stick to the Keto diet while eating delicious meals…Or maybe you'd just like to see a whole cookbook on brunch recipes or overnight breakfasts… You're the boss!

The only reason I can write cookbooks and try new recipes for a living is because of you, so now is my time to show some gratitude by creating cookbooks that will actually help you get through your weekly meals or special occasions! Just let us know what you'd like to see more of, and you can bet we'll get your ideas to the drawing board.

Thanks,

Tristan

Printed in Great Britain
by Amazon